# Miss BJB

## Overcoming Mistaken Identity

Written by

## Djuana Monique Ross

Miss BJB – Overcoming Mistaken Identity

All Scripture quotations are taken from the King James Version (KJV) of the Bible. Copyright ©1989 by Thomas Nelson, Inc., Publishers

Published by Tru Story Publications

Printed by Create Space Publishing

ISBN: 978-0-692-96182-7

Book Cover Design by Djuana Ross
Interior Design by Djuana Ross
Silhouette Image of teens on Back Cover & Pledge created by Kjpargeter of Freepik.com
Author Photo by J Renee Creations

For more information, email DRoss@TruTalentProductions.com

# TABLE OF CONTENTS

## ACKNOWLEDGEMENTS

Thank you, God, for giving me a testimony and for allowing me to learn from my pain rather than be defeated by it. I pray that this book touches every person that simply needs to know that they matter.

## DEDICATION

I dedicate this book to every young person that I have ever taught that helped me to see that there is value in my life advice. Pay it forward, my babies!

# INTRODUCING MISS BJB

*"To know me is to love me; comprehension is the key."*
- *Djuana "Miss BJB" Ross*

What does "to know me is to love me" even mean? Simply put, it means that in order to value my awesomeness you would have to put in the time to understand who I truly am.

For the majority of my life, I have attempted to convince people to love me. More times than I'd like to count, I failed this mission. Friends, family, classmates, teachers, coworkers, bosses, students, neighbors, you name it have been the targets of my desperate efforts to obtain the love and acceptance that I felt I deserved, but I didn't have. I am sure that there were many reasons why I still did not matter to the people that I chose to love me, but I have finally discovered that the real problem was that these people simply did not know me.

The truth of the matter is that I have always felt invisible. No matter what I did or didn't do, people just seemed to not see or hear me. So, when I got to the place in my life when I definitely knew who I was and what I stood for it didn't seem to change my status of invisibility. Time after time, if

I were to look you square in the face and plainly tell you who I am…you still wouldn't know me. Though I was now comfortable in my true identity, I still didn't feel the love and acceptance I craved because it seemed like no one was listening. I was constantly left **feeling alone in a crowded room**. Have you ever felt like that?

The best way to describe this feeling is through the eyes of the very misunderstood BLACK JELLY BEAN. Think about it. Of all of the jelly beans in a bag, the black jelly bean has the worst reputation. *"No one likes the black ones"* I've heard people say when that brightly colored candy is offered. People make faces, disgusted noises, and proclaim myths as truths when describing what the black jelly bean tastes like. Though it does have the acquired taste of black licorice that it seems only that certain taste bud goes for, the treatment that the bean receives oftentimes is overkill. By no ways am I saying to eat black jelly beans if you've tried them and have decided that you just don't care for them. However, most claims of the black jelly bean's nastiness come from people who have never had their own experience tasting the bean itself.

Black jelly beans go under the most scrutiny before acceptance from a candy lover is achieved. It sticks out like a sore thumb because it looks different. Due to the darkness of its exterior, it is mistaken as ugly and unpopular. How horrible it is to cast away the jelly bean that is exactly like the other jelly beans in the bag because its different – it was manufactured in the same plant as the others, it is made of the same ingredients minus its color and flavor, and it is shaped identically as the rainbow colored jelly beans. The fact of the matter is that the black jelly bean is the most hated because it is the most misunderstood. Its unique characteristics make it a novelty for the open-minded, but it also makes it a target for intense dislike simply because most people do not take the time to taste the black jelly bean firsthand. This was exactly how I felt at sixteen years old and continued to feel as an adult. Miss-represented, Miss-judged, Miss-treated, Miss-understood… Does this sound like you?

As far back as I can remember people have always placed me in some box just like the black jelly bean. It is highly likely that even while I am bearing my soul and showing someone exactly who I am and what I'm made of in plain sight; the person would still place me into a single rinky-dink box. This has happened to me throughout my life over and over again. Most people probably have no problem with being labeled. I, however, abhor being categorized especially if I've been mislabeled. I tell you that I am not just one thing! I am not one signature characteristic with recessive traits that typically accompany a single dominant trait. The issue is not that I have trouble figuring out who I am, but rather people have proven to have issue with accepting that I am not who they peg me to be.

I hope to shed light on what it is like to be alone in a crowded room. Where people can see you, hear you, smell you, touch you yet still misunderstand you, reject you, ignore you and neglect you. Though many times it is not the fault of the 'black jelly bean' that they're misunderstood, I have painfully discovered that people like me have to work diligently to not perpetuate the perception that individuals who are different can't do XYZ. (XYZ = insert anything you can think of here) Through pain and hurt, the 'black jelly bean' must oftentimes feverishly fight their way to who they've been purposed to be by God. They have to overcome mistaken identity.

When it's all said and done, getting to truly know people is our duty as fellow human beings. We are to not only get to know people, but to love them. God is love. As people of the Most High, we have been commissioned to be like Him. A great start would be to learn one another, love one another and try to understand what and where people have come from. Take this journey with me as I reminisce on some of the good, the bad and the ugly of my life.

Everything that has ever happened to me happened for a reason. I believe that a lot of that reason is so that I can share with others that may one day face some of the same things that I did. Furthermore, they can have another example of someone who overcame troubles, someone who triumphed in spite of trials and tribulation. It may be that you see yourself or a loved one in some of these accounts. In the event that you do, please know that you are not alone. It has oftentimes brought me comfort just to know that someone else can relate to what I may be feeling or going through.

It is my intention to share aspects of my life that have taught me valuable life lessons. Within these pages you'll ascertain truths that I learned through observation, unwelcome victimization and willful participation. The scripture in Revelation 12:11 (KJV) says that you *"overcome by the word of their testimony"*. I believe that others can be set free, delivered and armed with information through my life's examples. This book has not been written to air out dirty laundry, nor is it to gain fame from my misfortunes. I want to let my light so shine that men may see God's good works and glorify my Father in heaven. (Matthew 5:16).

As my high school history teacher, Mr. VonBerg, used to tell people, "DJ Sanders tells it like it tis!" Here we go, I am bringing it to you straight, no sugar! To know me is to love…comprehension is the key!

I would like to formally introduce to you … **Miss BJB**.

**Be Yourself** in the face of every challenge!

*-Djuana "Miss BJB" Ross*

# DESTINED 2B DIFFERENT

*"Be Yourself...Everyone Else Is Already Taken."-Oscar Wilde*

It was Inauguration Day... Djuana Monique Sanders was technically born on *"a day observed to bring about the beginning of"* - that is its definition. I entered the world on Friday, January 20, 1984 at 2:01pm. It seems that the numbers 1, 2, 0 are definitely assigned to my destiny (birth date - 1/20; birth time - 2:01; birth name – 20 letters) and explains why I tend to always give and want 120% in everything I do and am involved in. A day set aside to celebrate the beginning of a new era is the day God chose for my official debut... I was most certainly destined to be different.

The first gift that every baby receives is its name. You see, your name is what first identifies you from everyone else. What you will be called for the remainder of your life kind of determines your future. That is why many parents are very particular about what their precious baby will be named. Your name in some way or another can have a big impact on who it is you are to become. A name is a gift that keeps on giving.

One day I decided to research my name to get a better understanding of what people were calling me at a time where I was still trying to figure out my identity. My father gave me my first name, Djuana, and my maternal grandmother gave me my middle name, Monique. Through careful research, I found that Djuana Monique means *"gracious gift of God"* and *"advisor"*. I am a believer that nothing is just a coincidence. Everything that happens, happens for a reason. I don't believe that my father knew at the time what Djuana meant because his name is Dwayne, so I assume that he was probably just naming me after him. Little did he know, he was setting me up to be a child and servant of God that will be used as a gift under His grace.

My name has certainly shaped me into who I am now and who I was becoming when growing up. Now, I have never asked her, but I find it interesting that my grandmother chose a French name that means advisor. Why, interesting? Well, my family has only called me by my middle name. I have cousins that easily forget what my legal first name is if you ask them too quickly. No lie; one time my cousin listed me as an emergency contact for her daughter's school, who happens to be my goddaughter.

When I arrived to pick my godchild up, the secretary could not verify my identity because the closest name they could find was Monique Sims instead of what was on my ID which is Djuana Ross. I quickly explained that Monique is my middle name and that Sims is my maiden name. They released the child to me. I literally laugh out loud every time I think about it! It's not her fault because my family pretty much only knows me by my middle name. I can tell whether or not I am related to you based off of what you call me. So, all of my life my middle name has been activated. My relatives were not just calling me, "Monique", they have been calling me "Advisor".

**Advisor**. The irony is that I am most comfortable when I am in careers and roles where I can give people advice. Seriously, I have been giving people unsolicited advice since I was a child. Whenever I saw a need, I wanted to provide a workable solution. Go back with me to 1996 underneath the covering of the gymnasium on the playground of Cleveland School for the Arts on Pursell Avenue in Dayton, Ohio. There I was, a sixth grader, enjoying my extra recess. My classmates were running around playing football and basketball, climbing the monkey bars, playing 4 Square and hopscotch, and gossiping about the latest sixth grade news. You could find me setting up three chairs on the steps of the entrance into the school – one for me and two facing me for... my scheduled clients. That's right. When I learned that we were getting additional time for recess I decided that it was the perfect time to help a host of my classmates that were in high profile relationships with their obvious issues. No, really. This is what I decided to do with my extra play time. What was crazier is that of the six couples that had scheduled appointments, five of them actually sat in those chairs and listened to my advice! Even crazier than that... I didn't even have a boyfriend and hadn't even had a real one before! From that day to this one, I shine in the gift of giving others good advice. I mean, I am a teacher, a motivational speaker, a blogger, and a life coach... you see?

Being Djuana Monique is who I am. It just so happens that my name captures who I am becoming. Have you ever researched the meaning of your name? What are people calling you? I didn't know until recently, but since learning the research I have a stronger sense of who I am. I thank God for blessing me with family that intentionally or unintentionally gave me a name that I can be proud of. I absolutely LOVE my name, my gift! I love it so much that I even wrote a poem about it.

I know that I just put a whole lot of emphasis on names. The truth is that they are pretty important. Someone calling you a flattering nickname or calling you out of your name can bring about a reaction from you. When the reaction is being observed by others it shows them who you are, what you answer to. If everyone calls you "Doo Doo" then thoughts of nastiness, filth and bowel movements come to mind. On the flip, if your nickname is "Pretty Pauline" then thoughts of a beautiful looking girl come to mind who may even be colorful and bright like a parrot. I'm just saying…names are very important. As Madea said in one of those Tyler Perry films, *"it ain't about what they call you, it's what you answer to. You remember that. You hear me?"* And you are called, destined even, to be different!

According to my astrological sign, online personality tests, and observations of other uncanny characteristics, Djuana Monique has a strong urge to just be different. They say that I tend to walk to the beat of my own drum and prefer it that way. You know what? All of those sources are very correct! Now, you don't have to be born in January or even have a name that you are proud of like me. You are destined to be different just because God designed you different from everyone else. There is not another you nor has there ever been or will there ever be on this planet. God was very intentional with how He put you together. He knew you before you were born and He knows who you will be when your life's journey ends. You, too, are unique!

My life's journey consists of me actively seeking ways to be different because I have never, and I mean NEVER liked being like someone else. In my hallway hangs a framed artwork of a crimson and silver vanity with the words **"Be yourself – everyone else is already taken"** written on the mirror. I was excited to find a photo that beautifully expresses what has been my life's mission. Even as a little girl when playing house with my brother and the neighborhood kids I did not want to play the mother just because I was the only girl. I was uncomfortable fitting into a box at five years old. The same remains true today at the age of thirty-three. Dr. Seuss says, *"Why fit in when you were born to stand out?"* Wise words, indeed.

It is okay to not be like everyone else. The onset of puberty, puberty itself, and preparing to enter adulthood are some of the most trying times to your identity that you may experience. It's not easy to be a young person. People like to try you. They want to see what you're about. They want to see where you stand. For some, they don't even know yet. For others, they may not have the courage to "be me" when being me is not deemed as cool. I am here to tell you that it is totally worth being yourself at all costs. Peer pressure is strong, but it is not invincible. No one can force you to do things that you don't want to do. No one can force you to say things that you really don't want to say. No one can force you to be friends with people that do not believe what you believe. It's all on you. It is okay to be yourself. As a matter of fact, the world NEEDS you to be yourself. If you're not you, then who is?

Trust me, you are brave enough to be yourself right now. When I was three years old, my very first career aspiration was to be a background dancer for Michael Jackson. Oh my goodness, I was serious, too, even at that age! His influence helped grow my love of music and I discovered that I wanted to become a singer. Now everybody wanted to be a singer when I was younger, so that wasn't very different. However, I was different in how I approached my dream. I started a singing group with two of my best friends when I was ten years old. We wrote our own songs, had our own choreography and our own style. I remember wanting to name the group Bad Girls, but found out that that name had already been taken so we chose B.A.D. GALS. Lol, so different, I know. B.A.D. stood for our names: Brittany. Ashley. Djuana. I truly wanted us to make it. I wrote my own press by creating a magazine on the computer my father had bought me from the military base. It was a music magazine that featured my group in an interview and lyrics to our newest song. I wrote articles about what was going on in music at the time, as well as, locally. I only had one issue, but it helped me materialize my dream. You have to understand that this happened in 1994, the internet was new and there was no such thing as a search engine or an app. I was years before my time, I tell you.

I was determined to be a big singing superstar in the music industry, but I have always been a realist. No matter how kids loved me on the playground, I found out that I was an okay singer, but there were people my age that were just way better than me. So, instead of letting that realization crush my dream, my dream evolved.

My dream evolved, at the age of twelve, into me wanting my own record label. I wanted to put other great acts on the map. That became my new dream! I researched and followed the careers of singer-songwriters and Berry Gordy, in particular. I wanted to be the female Berry Gordy at this point. Just like him, I wanted my own music empire! No, I'm not a Cookie or Lucious from the television show Empire, but I was very serious. I named my first label DJWorks Records and I was excited. I did not know anybody my age that wanted a record label; thus, I felt great because I still had my dream my way, different from everyone else. I made being different my life's goal. I may be similar to others, but I wanted to be me. I wanted to create an empire that everyone would one day remember and know that Djuana Monique had been here.

Why? Because I just enjoy being different! I thrive on it! My very existence rests on it. It is my identity. It's what makes me so special. You are special, too. Why be like anyone else? Your identity is yours. Just like a fingerprint is so unique that no one in the world will ever have it, so are you. Get comfortable in your own skin. Get to know your name and what you like to answer to. Be you! Sprinkle your essence on the world! God made you, and God didn't make no junk! Know yourself so that you can love yourself. From this day forward... JUST BE YOU, DIFFERENT AND ALL!

**MISS BJB AFFIRMATION:**

*I am who I am comfortably and I absolutely love my identity. It is necessary for me to be me so that I can leave my unique mark on the world. I, boldly, will be different and stand out amongst the crowds.*

# Miss Me – The Misconception

*"Wisdom is the principal thing; therefore get wisdom:*
*and with all thy getting get understanding."*

*– Proverbs 4:7 KJV*

To know me is to love…comprehension is the key.

If I could summarize the purpose of this book into one chapter, it would be this one!  My entire life has felt like a fight to truly be heard, to be seen and to just be accepted for who I am.  I identify as Miss BJB for this very reason.  I have explained what the BJB represents…Black Jelly Bean.  However, the Miss in this moniker is just as important.  I know that it just looks like a title and when discovering this name for myself it definitely made sense as I was a single young woman at the time.  But let us take a closer look at the word Miss…

The Merriam-Webster dictionary defines the word *miss* as a transitive verb meaning…

1. To fail to hit, reach, or contact
2. To discover or feel the absence of
3. To fail to obtain
4. Escape, avoid
5. To leave out, omit

6.        To fail to comprehend, sense, or experience

7.        To fail to perform or attend

Now, I know that may seem like a lot of definitions, but there's more. When searching for the definition in Google they define the word *miss* as a verb AND a noun. There are only a few of the many definitions listed on Google that I want to focus on as others are similar to what is stated in the Merriam-Webster dictionary. I particularly like the word choices used to formulate the definitions.

Google says that the word, *miss* means…

1.        Be too late to catch

2.        Fail to notice, hear or understand

3.        Fail to see or have a meeting with

4.        Not be able to experience or fail to take advantage of

5.        Notice the loss of absence of

You may be able to make the connections on your own, but I think it'll be most beneficial for me to explore and expound on this a bit further. Explain to you why I am Miss BJB… I have suffered a lot of pain and heartache in my life primarily because I feel like no one understands me. Even the most loving people in my life don't fully comprehend me as a person. I admit I'm a simply complex person, but I just don't believe I'm that difficult to understand. Consequently, I struggled with my identity because as I was growing into who I really am people made me feel like that person was inadequate, unworthy and just weird.

How do my emotional issues relate to a bunch of definitions of a single word? Made plain in black and white one can see that the word miss is heavy. Just look at these definitions. The words, **FAIL TO,** are littered throughout. Fail to understand or comprehend. Fail to see, notice, hear, experience, attend, perform, obtain, reach, contact, hit, catch, discover...My GOD! That doesn't even touch the definitions that state to leave out or omit, escape and avoid. Miss is a loaded word with heavy connotations. That word truly describes how I've felt throughout my life and why I am writing this book.

It reminds me of this one time when...

I was standing in the middle of my mother's living room, I remember being completely flabbergasted, as she told me about myself. My memory only replays the phrases that impacted me most. It went something like this...

*"You think you're better than us just because you're a lighter skinned. You ain't better than nobody. There's always someone better than you, honey. Remember that. [...] You're a bitch!"*

My mouth fell wide open. She angrily walked up the stairs as my emotions went into complete shock. I was in utter disbelief as the woman that I loved and who raised me with everything she had emphatically expressed her opinion of me at that moment with total disgust and almost a hateful passion. I was completely blindsided by her comments and these statements left permanent scars on my emotional and psychological being. **Now before you take this scenario and run wild in your imaginations with it,** let me explain a bit more as to what was going on here AND who I have learned my mother to be.

First of all, it is important for you to understand that I was no angel growing up. I was not a horribly behaved child either, but definitely not an angel 100% all of the time. So the entire soliloquy that my mother presented that day was definitely in response to something I did or said. I honestly do not remember what actions I'd taken or words that I'd spoken to provoke these specific comments and then some. I do remember that this encounter that I am reminiscing about happened when I was around age twelve or thirteen. Though I cannot recall what my fault was in this exact moment I can say that like MANY teenagers at this stage of life, I'm pretty sure I just may have been "smelling myself", as the older generation calls it. *("Smelling yourself" means that you are under the impression that you are at a higher level than what you truly are. Typically this phrase is used to describe children who were acting "grown" or disrespectful for their age.)* Nevertheless, my mother totally crushed my soul that day! She did not play that and demanded respect from her children. That's just the way it was and is to this day.

I literally was crushed to my core as I swallowed the words that spewed out of her mouth. I stood there digesting what she'd said about me over and over. I just couldn't stomach it, but the words kept reverberating in my mind. For whatever indiscretion I may have been guilty, maybe I needed to be brought down a peg or three and I may have needed some stern correction, but what was hard to swallow was the overall tone and her word choice used to put me in my place. It's like the words *"you think you're better than us"* and *"you're a bitch"* were stuck in my throat and had starting choking the life out of me. A certain part of me began to die that day.

The question, *"Is this really what my mother thought of me?"* was bouncing around my head for a long time. I had been blindsided by my mother's perception of me and it hurt. It hurt me deeply because even when I was "smelling myself", I had NEVER thought I was better than any member of my family. They were all that I had and I loved them beyond the moon and sky. Not only did I <u>not</u> think that highly of myself, I certainly wouldn't have felt that way due to my skin color. Consequently, I was super confused! I was lighter than my mother and brother as a result of my father's genes who is a light - skinned man, but I never cared about that. It was so left field that I was left speechless.

Seriously, where on earth did my mother come to this outlandish conclusion that in any of my words or actions - from birth to that point - I thought that I was better than the people I loved? I did not understand why this was said or where it had come from at all. It hurt so badly because it was the farthest thing from the truth. As if that wasn't painful enough, like being hit by a mach truck, my own mother had ended her soliloquy by calling me a bitch. Now I know for a fact that whatever I'd done that day did not equate to me being called something so derogatory, especially at the age of twelve or thirteen. Reflecting back on this scenario, no matter what I'd did I wasn't that bad or disrespectful. I just wasn't.

What I was, though, was sensitive. The consequence for words that cannot be unspoken from that definitive moment has shaped me both positively and negatively. Already dealing with low self-esteem for various reasons, I now began to deal with feeling completely unloved by everyone in my life including my own mother. Now, don't get it twisted. I now know that people loved me, but at that time I was so fragile that situations like this only pushed me further into the dark, deep recesses of my mind. This is a vivid example of how misunderstanding one's actions can cause significant damage. A ripple effect created out of this helped to mold a seemingly normal, young preteen into a later self-doubting, low self-esteem having young person who emotionally withdrew from others to protect herself from further hurtful exchanges as a result of misunderstanding her character, personality, or actions. All in all, I felt completely rejected at that point.

Many years later, I realized a few things. One – that my mother was human and was capable of making mistakes. Though it hurt to hear the words that came out of her mouth, I have no real clue as to what could have been going in her mind at the time nor can I fully comprehend what it must have been like to be her in shoes at that time. Two – I did not remain stuck in the past. Just because it hurt that day did not mean that I was to remain hurt at thirty three years old. It was imperative that I forgive the sting, learn the lesson, and move on. Three – there will always be times when life throws you a knockdown punch, but remember that you are down and not out. Forgive to move on, and remember to teach others. Had this not happened, I would not know how to unapologetically be myself when peer pressure arises. This situation taught me that I can take the negative words that anyone could say about me because I survived hurtful words from the woman I loved the most. No one else had the power to hurt me like she did, and I did not break. Truth be told moments like what I went through with my mother have the potential to completely break a person. It took me a long time to rediscover my worth and have a better understanding of what took place that afternoon.

I wish that I had known at that age to take a step back and thoroughly understand that there were two conversations going on at that time for me to analyze. The first conversation was indeed the facts that I laid out in previous paragraphs, but the second one was the inner conversation that I was having with myself. I had yet to learn that it was my responsibility to reject those words that truly did not represent me. It was my job to turn away from those words that countered my true identity. It did not matter who spoke these words over my identity, I was to ferociously protect my self-worth by inwardly rejecting what was not true. Had I'd known to do that, I would have avoided many years of tension headaches, chest pains, self-love issues, depression, self-sabotage, and even suicidal thoughts. I may not have known then, but I am grateful that I know now!

How many people do you know that feel like the word *miss*? You see, I grew up poor and in the projects in a single parent home in the inner city. That was hard enough, but when you add on the weight of being Miss BJB it oftentimes makes me give God praise that I'm even still alive! I may not have a lot of made-for-TV horror stories that shaped my life, but the internal struggle of just being recognized on a day-to-day basis was excruciatingly painful.

When I think about it, I just wanted someone to get to know me for real. I had usually been pigeon-holed as "one thing" and not considered as a whole, well-rounded person with different levels to my being. As a child, I was labeled a nerd because I liked school, had good grades, and wore glasses. I was way more than that because I was also heavy into hip hop, loved watching people fight, and was actually kind of ghetto. As a teenager, I was labeled the "church girl" and "Mama Djuana" because I had a serious relationship with Jesus Christ and walked out what I preached. My fellow classmates and even church-going saints often neatly placed me into this goody two shoes box that only cared about doing the right thing. Though that was a big part of who I was, many people did not take into consideration that I was also dealing with my hormones, desperately wanted a boyfriend, and just wanted someone to choose me to hang out or have fun sometimes. Labels are such a trap, but it became my mission to not accept what others see or say about me. I had to make sure that I knew who I was in totality even if others didn't.

When people weren't taking hold of one aspect of my character, they were completely ignoring me. No other reason made sense for why people couldn't fully capture my essence. There were times when people would flat out lie about who I was despite the fact that it didn't fit any iota of my personality at all. When I wasn't being ignored, I was being misinterpreted. I am a pretty straight forward person, but that has still not stopped people from creating these narratives about me or my personality that are the complete opposite of who I am. It can be annoying and heartbreaking. It's heartbreaking because I don't fully understand how a person can believe these made-up versions of me when I am such an open book and they could see for themselves that whatever they heard was obviously not true.

***I am not a horrible person. I'm just so misunderstood that my love, my person gets ignored and devalued.***

Honestly, I have millions of examples in every stage of my life where I have literally said something to an individual or a group that claimed they didn't hear me, but when a different person would say the EXACT same thing I did the very next moment they would receive the acknowledgement. The reoccurring encounter would always leave me feeling bewildered and invisible. I thought that my speaking voice must be extremely low, so I worked on projecting my voice. Let me tell you that the same experience continued to happen. After many years of conducting this unofficial experiment, I concluded that people didn't WANT to hear me. That had to be it because I would look them right in their faces and project my voice so that whatever I said was heard, but nothing. It's still hard to grapple with. I can relate to anyone that has the communication issues that I have with others. I know the damaging effects that miscommunication can have on sensitive, young people like myself.

When you know you're not being heard you begin to feel worthless. I still fight off the following thoughts: *"what is the point?"* and *"I don't matter anyway."* It can be very difficult to deal with. It usually leads to issues in self-esteem/self-worth, depression, and even suicidal thoughts. To feel alone in this big world – or just in a crowded room – sucks. It just does.

To be misunderstood feels horrible, so how do I combat the damaging issues that come with it? By choosing to know yourself first. It may feel unfair, but so is life. Learn who you are so that others cannot inaccurately shape who they think you are. It can be difficult, but it's worth it. If I could do it; believe me, you can do it, too!

It is not easy being yourself because there is a chance that others, even those that love you, will misjudge who you are. It can even be risky to your living comfort level, but very necessary to protect who you truly are. You may have to go to war in your mind and fight for clarity of your identity. Having peace of mind and spirit is important when living life at any age. When others misconceive who you are it can bring on many negative thoughts, but you can overcome them. Be sure to know that you matter even if no one understands you. Combat misconceptions with the truth. God's word says that you are fearfully and wonderfully made. He says that He knew you before you knew yourself. He says that you are above and not beneath. He says that no weapon formed against you will prosper. He says that you can do all things through Christ that strengthens you. Use God's truth to reset your mind when you're attacked with a misconception. Affirm yourself with positive thoughts and set a solid foundation in your identity.

**MISS BJB AFFIRMATION:**

*I will fight for my true identity. The words and actions of others will not change my being, but it is allowed to positively shape my being. No matter how misunderstood, misinterpreted, or misrepresented that I may be, I will ALWAYS strive to be ME!*

# K(NO)W NEGATIVITY

*"Death and life are in the power of the tongue: and they that love it shall eat the fruit thereof.*

*– Proverbs 18:21 KJV*

One of the number one reasons I feel like a black jelly bean is because of the seeds that others planted in me as a child. The words from others shaped my view of myself and my view of the world. Though I can honestly respect the fact that the adults that were around me as a child were still figuring life out or were still young themselves or were just dealt a "bad hand", it does not negate the fact that their mistakes and their negativity wore off on me, wore me out and also wore me down.

When I was about 5 years old, I remember crying in response to something that my mother said to me. Whatever it was, it hurt my little feelings. She told me to stop crying. My mother wasn't necessarily the nurturing type so when she told me to stop crying it wasn't your "Cosby Show"/"Family Matters" TV show moment where a big hug is given along with the moral of the lesson. It came out harsh...for a 5 year old anyway. This particular time my grandmother was nearby. She spoke up on my behalf (I didn't say a word...we were taught to be respectful and to stay in a child's place no matter what). My grandmother told my mother to stop saying that and explained to her that I was sensitive. I remember the moment my grandmother told my mother that I was sensitive because that was the moment in my life that let me know that I was not "wrong" for my feelings. I had a lot of them, feelings that is. I felt as though whenever I let my feelings show I was being corrected not to. It perplexed me and made me feel wrong. It's as if my feelings defined who I was and if I wasn't allowed to express them then I felt as though I had no identity. Yes, even at 5 years old.

*Sensitive.* Yes, that is definitely one of my main characteristics. That day was the day I realized that my grandmother was truly my ally. She understood me. As I grew older, this still holds to be true. In a world full of people and I have met thousands I'm sure...my grandmother is one of the only people on earth that just gets me. Many people love me, care for me and are on my team, BUT not many of those same people understand a quirky, different person like me.

And what people don't understand, they criticize. They judge. They try to change. They put down. I almost don't believe many people do these things on purpose. It has been the way of the world since before Jesus walked the earth. Negativity has been adopted as a norm in our society and the consequences of injecting negativity into the veins of children or young people is severely dangerous.

Let me break down a bit. It was the little things that people said or didn't say to me that hurt the most. I may be sensitive, but I had to develop thick skin very early in life. Life can be difficult and patience can wear out which causes frustration. In all fairness, for the most part I understood why so many people in my life were negative. At certain times in my life I felt like I got negativity from all sides, for real. It was coming from the teachers at school, my classmates and friends, neighbors and family members, strangers, even members of the church…it was everywhere. Negativity bore down on me. It got so bad that as I grew into adulthood, I even took on a lot of those same negative attitudes and behaviors that hurt me growing up. Truthfully, the only reason I changed from a lot of those learned behaviors is because there were a few totally honest people throughout my life that put it in my face and told me I was negative.  Unbeknownst to me at the time, I was becoming the very thing I hated.  I had to change.

Growing up in a low-income housing authority – aka the projects – has a way of influencing your way of doing things no matter who you are.  My family had a wealth of great characteristics such as compassion, generosity, humor, cooking and cleaning, but the environment that my relatives were bred crept into their personalities, too.  Several of my relatives, including myself, have been guilty of dismissing people who are different, cutting people off by "not being bothered", engaging in self-damaging habits such as smoking and drinking, and speaking very pessimistically about everything.  The latter has had the most influence in my personality development.  Unknowingly, I could find the problem in everything including compliments given to me.  Someone would say to me, "you look really nice today" and I would counter it with a put-down like "my outfit was only four dollars".  Honestly, I had adopted a common trait that ran rampant through my family and hadn't even noticed.

As in the example, I was not only negative about others, but also about myself.  I spoke very negatively about myself without thought. Your words have power and I was literally killing my identity with negativity. After some good-natured people brought this well-practiced habit to my attention I began my journey into unchartered territory.

I started taking responsibility for my attitudes and asked God to change me into who He would want me to be. Closer inspection showed me that I could place the blame of my funky ways onto so many others. I could point and say that it was so and so's fault that I am the way that I am. However, God showed me that JUST BECAUSE I was exposed to and even taught the ways of negative thinking, attitudes and behaviors DID NOT mean that gave me license to take any of that on in my life now. I was responsible for what I did with the negativity that I'd been given and taught. God placed the ball back in my court and said, "What are you going to do with it?"

Today, I ask you, **"What are you going to do with the negativity that's been hurled at you?"**

I decided a long time ago that I would be the voice (like my grandmother was for me) for those who can't speak on their own behalf. I decided to learn what NOT to do, how NOT to act and how NOT to be from the very same negative experiences that were designed to tear me down or show me how to tear down others. When I finally figured out how to undo some of the damage and learned ways, I took on this mission to educate and enlighten young people to combat negativity head on. In my opinion, the future ramifications of others' negativity are too grave as it affects so much of a person's life. I don't want young people having to make the same mistakes that I did. I want them to be equipped with the right stuff so that they have a better chance at being whole and living a balanced life.

I don't know why many adults (parents, teachers, authority figures, strangers, etc.) don't understand that what you say to a child WILL greatly impact them in their future. Death and life are truly in the tongue! There's no excuse sufficient enough to justify why some adults are super negative and nasty with children and young people! Tough love and discipline are necessary, but when drenched in negativity it's damaging. Though there are several factors that can be considered, and certainly if studied case by case, one can wholeheartedly break down and understand why things are said or take a turn for the worse when trying to raise a child today. Nevertheless, make no mistake that the Word of God is true. If you use your tongue to speak death or negativity over someone, you will see that fruit come forth later. All adults need to be mindful of how you speak to EVERY child and young person you encounter. Death and life are in your tongue and these children will become what you speak of and to them.

Furthermore, if you have been the recipient of negativity and it can cause you to be a shell of the person that you really are. Meaning you can become someone you do not want to be. **I need you to UNLEARN what you've been taught. FORGIVE any and everyone that brought you pain. BE BETTER than your examples have been to you.** In some cases, it may not have been your fault for however you're turning out to be. However, it is YOUR RESPONSIBILITY to take the good out of the bad. It is YOUR RESPONSIBILITY, just as it was mine, to learn what NOT to do, how NOT to be and how NOT to act. Truth be told, only YOU can control how you will be.

Just because someone spoke death over you doesn't mean that you're supposed to accept it. **Turn that thing around and speak LIFE over the death that others have tried to put on you.** Even I didn't realize that those seeds of "how I was raised" and being a "product of my environment" had sprouted into these weeds that were choking the life out of my life. I finally learned that negativity given to me was not an excuse for me to spew negativity, hate or hurt onto the rest of the world. Bottom line: HURT PEOPLE HURT PEOPLE.

So, let's stop the cycle…say no to negativity even if you know negativity. You know what I mean?

**MISS BJB AFFIRMATION:**

*Today is the day that I will give the stiff arm to any words of negativity that have the potential to injure me instead of grow me. I will speak life into my life and commit to knowing that there is <u>no excuse</u> for being negative.*

# SUICIDE IS SERIOUS

*"Yea, though I walk through the valley of the shadow of death,*
*I will fear no evil: for thou art with me..."*
*– Psalm 23:4a*

By far the toughest day of my teaching career was the day that a staff member casually handed me a folded piece of paper...

I don't remember all of the details, but I remember walking outside of my classroom door to read the half page letter that the school administration had typed up for all staff to read immediately. The first line that I read stated that on March 2, 2012 a student passed away. I read the name of the student and tears immediately poured from my eyes. Not only was the ninth-grader a member of the student body, but she was one of <u>my</u> babies that I'd taught just last semester. Everything else the note stated went over my head, but somehow my eyes zoomed in on the words "possible suicide." Right then, I couldn't breathe.

The hardest part of anyone dying suddenly is that "I <u>just</u> saw them!" feeling. Not two day prior to this note, I had seen her. The school had an assembly and all high-schoolers were present. I was on deck to help with seating and that's the first time I'd seen my dear since before Christmas break. She seemed "normal" to me when I taught her – full of life. Seeing her briefly at the assembly, I noticed no change. It still bothers me that I was wrong.

Before I knew it the school's regularly scheduled program was accommodating for in-school grief counseling for any student that needed it. She was a beautiful young lady that touched the lives and hearts of many students. The halls were very somber for days. A night vigil was coordinated in her memory and I attended. It was heart-warming to see the turnout, but heart-wrenching to accept the reason why we were there. According to the words of her relatives and youth pastor, they saw no sign of this coming. My heart was just sick. How come it seemed like no one had picked up on this? Why couldn't anyone that knew her see that she wanted her life to end? I had no answers and truthfully, I still don't.

Listening to her loved ones, I had learned that it was no one's fault. They did not want any of her peers or anyone thinking that there was something that they could have done to reverse what had already been done. I needed to hear that because I, personally, was struggling.

I was struggling with her death because at different times in my own life that could have been me. Two things happened to me as a result of this child's suicide. One – I vowed that day to always trust my spirit and simply ASK if a person was okay. You sincerely have no idea what another person may be dealing with. It is my belief that showing someone you care enough to hear whether or not they are okay can save a life. It can give them hope that maybe they can make it another day. I know this to be true because from that day to this one I have talked to SEVERAL students that revealed to me that they contemplated suicide at one point or another. I never would have known had I not asked them how they were.

I wasn't able to prevent one student's death, but by the leading of the Lord He has helped me to prevent others. He has used me as a vessel to give help, hope and a listening ear to students that were considering running away or were self-medicating or were cutting. All of those conversations kept me on the front-lines of teaching. When paperwork, politics and behaviors become too much for me, I think about my passion to protect students from themselves, especially those that may be having self-harming or suicidal thoughts.

Two – I was forced to deal with my own history of suicidal thoughts. Many of the different factors in my life left me feeling inadequate at times, like I was never enough. Since the age of five, whenever life was particularly hard for me I would slip into the "George Bailey" mode. In the movie, *It's A Wonderful Life,* the main character – George Bailey - believes that everyone would be better off if he had never been born. That's the "George Bailey" syndrome as I have called it. Many times I would just wish I had never been born and I meant it.

I was never bold enough to try to actually kill myself, but in my thoughts I was dying in many different ways. Though my thoughts were only suicidal sporadically, it was still a problem even in my adulthood. This tragic event had caused me to address my thought life. I had to recognize the importance of how thoughts turn to action if you don't reject them. It was time to change my thinking before my self-destructive thoughts became a reality, too.

By taking time to address my suppressed hurts, I began to heal. Prayer is my strongest tool! The biggest revelation from addressing this subject in my life was learning that I struggled with suicide because I am a target. The enemy aka the devil wants to kill me. Yes, that's right. He wants to kill me and anyone that is powerful. This thing is bigger than depression and circumstances and emotions. I figured out why so many of our young people are attacked with these thoughts and it is just that. He wants to take you out of the game so that you won't change it! He can't physically kill you so he attacks the mind and deceives you into thinking that no one wants you or loves you. He is such a liar! Don't give in to his temptations! What I didn't realize growing up is that somebody in this world needs me. I have found that many young people that struggle with suicidal thoughts are just like me. They don't realize that they are needed.

Why are these thoughts happening to you or someone you love? If they are not suffering from a mental illness, then it is because God knows that their experience will free and comfort someone else. Young people want to know that they are being heard and that someone understands.

Unfortunately, some of us know all too well and are able to relate to those that may presently be suffering.

I know that for some people this may be a difficult chapter to read, but suicide is serious. It's real out here. Suicide is happening way too often among our youth. I need you to know that suicide is NOT a fad and in some cases it is not even a psychological disorder. It is a supernatural attack that can only be battled and triumphed supernaturally. We need to pray! We need to battle in this spiritual warfare until victory is attained!

Black jelly beans are susceptible to suicidal thoughts because of the rejection, neglect, and fear of never being understood. It doesn't mean that all young people are struggling with this, but we need to stay in prayer and ask God to show us when someone needs Him to step in.

I want anyone reading this that may be struggling with self-harming behavior or a suicidal thought life to know this:

**SOMEONE LOVES YOU! SOMEONE NEEDS YOU!**

Many of my students, nieces, nephews, family and friends would have been sincerely hurt and outright mad if I hadn't kept living, if I'd believed the lie that I didn't matter.

IF YOU LEAVE, WHO WILL OTHERS IN YOUR POSITION HAVE TO RELATE TO FOR STRENGTH, COURAGE, AND WISDOM? Though I am not proud of my struggle, I have been able to use it to help others. The more I help someone else, the more healed I become.

**PRAYER WORKS!** Dagnabbit, call on God for help! He hears you, I promise! Please don't just check out of here because life is hard. You have purpose on this earth. Live it out and let God take you when you've completed it. Pray every time you need help!

I love you and I pray you understand how serious suicide is and help someone or yourself today. Keep living!

**MISS BJB AFFIRMATION:**

*I matter! I was given life so that I can <u>live it</u> and one day will leave a great legacy in the world. I matter!*

# LIVING WITH LOSS

*"When my father and my mother forsake me, then the Lord will take me up." – Psalm 27:10 KJV*

I can still taste her potato salad, her cheeseburgers made with bell peppers and onion, and even her hot dogs. My mind goes back to the plaits in her hair, her dentures in the plastic yellowish-orange cup, and the giant Jesus statute in the corner of her bedroom. My ears tingle with the way she would tell her age – "sweet sixteen", the way she would cuss someone out when she felt it necessary, and her signature melody… *"I love you a bushel and a peck; a bushel and a peck and a hug around the neck, a hug around the neck!"* She called me, "Tootsie" and I called her, "Mama". Sarah Sanders was one of my angels on earth, my great-grandmother.

The day she died truly rocked my world. The rock of my family had passed on April 11, 1999 and that day marks the day that my strength went to a whole new level. At fifteen years old, I faced one of the biggest losses of my life. At that point, I had only lost my neighbor and distant cousin on my father's side when I was twelve. When Chrissy died her death literally brought me to my knees and I barely had a real relationship with her. She was killed by knife in a fight with a girl over a boy while skipping school. But, Mama and I had a close relationship. She was very influential in shaping my life. I loved visiting her and her cooking always brought the family together. It had even been told to me that she said that "I was blessed" when I was born. Every moment that I spent with her was special and I miss her dearly. Dealing with the death of a loved one is never easy.

Unfortunately, people in our lives are going to die. I have since lost distant relatives, my paternal grandparents, a classmate to a drug overdose, teachers to cancer, and students to suicide or violence. What makes it difficult sometimes is that people tend to not properly teach young people how to handle death, or how to properly grieve. My great-grandmother's passing changed the dynamics of my life. Now that she's gone, my family is not that close at all. Shoot, I haven't seen my one of uncles since the funeral! Also, I had a huge new void... who else was I going to confide in? Who else was going to make me feel as special as she did? Who else was going to be as tender with me as she was?

You may be facing these same questions when someone you love dies and you are left feeling alone or even hopeless. I am here to tell you that you will never get over their loss, but you can live on through their memory. Use those precious moments to help you get through life. Don't allow your grief to stop your growth. Instead honor your loved ones by using their memory to fuel you, to fuel your will to live.

It is important for you to know that grief can and will take as long as it is going to take. Everyone grieves differently and that is perfectly normal. I encourage you to grieve by feeling. Yes, by feeling. YOU HAVE TO FEEL. IT IS NECESSARY FOR YOU TO FEEL! TAKE YOUR TIME. It is OKAY to have emotions and feel free to be yourself. If you cry, then cry. If you are angry, then be angry. If you are quiet, then be quiet. If you need to talk your way through it, then talk your way through it. As long as you're not being destructive to yourself or others, freely grieve in the way that works for you. There is no right way to grieve. Just don't be out here trying to numb the pain by self-medicating or taking out your pain on others unfairly.

I mentioned earlier that my strength went to a whole new level when Mama died. It did. I had to remain strong when writing her obituary. I had to keep it together as I sang *"Soon I Will Be Done"* at her funeral. I had to appear calm for my younger sibling and cousins as we faced her casket. When the "show" of the funeral was over though, I was left feeling abandoned. I felt like no one understood and never would the way she did. My identity was under attack because my cheerleader was gone. But, when thoughts of her awesomeness come to mind I remember that she is STILL my cheerleader! She is not here in body, but she has never left me in spirit. The same thing goes for you. **YOU ARE NOT ALONE.** Your loved one still loves you. Your loved one wants you to live abundantly. Be strong when loss happens. Hold onto your identity even in the midst of unmatched pain.

While you're learning how to cope with their loss, God always makes sure to send someone else to fill that void. Do not mistake me! The new person does NOT replace your loved one, but fills the gaping hole that losing them created. I am a living testimony that when the closeness in my family went away because of my great-grandmother's death, God sent me various "aunties" and "uncles" in the form of teachers, mentors, and even students. To this day, I never know how it happens, but I know that God sent me "family" whenever I am at my lowest. Just because I love them so much, please excuse me as I shout out a few of my "family".

Thank you, God for sending these people into my life as I tried to live with loss:

- Mrs. Madeline Green – *my elementary school choir and piano teacher later colleague*

- Mrs. Pamela Miller – *my elementary school friend's mom*

- Elder and Mrs. James R. Willis, Sr. – *my childhood church's pastor and his wife*

- Elder Timothy and Mrs. Margo Willis – *my childhood church family*

- The Dredden family – *my childhood church family turned extended family*

- Mr. Eric VonBerg – *my high school history teacher and student government advisor*

- Ms. Janice Cook and Ms. Theresa Rowan – *the mothers of my high school best friends*

- Dr. Donna Cox – *my college professor, boss, and mentor*

- Mrs. Jeannie Smith & Mrs. Cheryl Kochendorfer – *my college work supervisors*

- Denise Rehg – *my boss for my Culture Works internship*

- Darius, Ivory, DeMara, Jade & Jewel, Rhej'a, Antoinette, Devanney, Matt A., Chyna & Jadon – *my former students*

- Liz Whipps – *my high school magnet director turned work supervisor and my cheerleader*

- Jermaine J. Ross – *my best friend turned love of my life aka my husband*

I guarantee if you take an inventory of the people in your life, you will find that there is SOMEBODY there that loves you! You can conquer your pain and live with loss. You may never stop grieving, but you can live because you are blessed. Honor your loved ones by living a life that they'll be proud of.

## MISS BJB AFFIRMATION:

*I have not been abandoned even when loved ones leave. I recognize that they are with me in spirit and their memory is my strength when I am low. God has never and will never leave me. I am strong!*

# BEATING BETRAYAL

*"A man that hath friends must shew himself friendly;
and there is a friend that sticketh closer than a brother."*

*–Proverbs 18:24 KJV*

Nothing hurts more than when someone stabs you in the back. It is so unexpected and you're never really prepared for it. I mean, it's happening behind you, not in front where you can see. Being a teenager is hard enough trying to figure out your own identity while simultaneously having to keep your eye out for snakes in the grass and wolves in sheep's clothing. It is increasingly more difficult to notice them in your peers than it is among the well-known bullies and the obvious mean people.

Making and keeping true friends while developing into the person you want to be is a rite of passage every single person on the planet will encounter. You better believe that if you sit down and ask your elders to tell you how they handled a friend turning on them, they are guaranteed to have a story. Since humans are flawed and have been since Adam ate that forbidden fruit, in one way or another no matter who you are, you will have to deal with a backstabber even if that backstabber is you!

The word betrayal always sounds so diabolical to me. You can see examples of it happening in reality television shows like it's going out of style. However, the real reality is that the act of betraying has layers and is not so melodramatic all the time. It's not always a Jerry Springer -"you are not the father" Maury Povich - come to Dr. Phil situation that needs to be mediated by Judge Judy. Sometimes it's as simple as the friend that you confided in telling your secret when they promised to keep it on the hush. I'm sure that at this time in your life, you may have already experienced it or have been entangled in one of the levels of betrayal.

I've been there. As a matter of fact, I've been in both seats: the BETRAY - ED and the BETRAY - ER. No matter which role you play, the consequences are usually pretty painful and damaging. Do not be fooled by people that always claim that they don't ever get hurt by what others do or say. They're lying! No man is an island and we were designed by God to desire to be with others that can help us be fruitful and multiply. (No, I'm not just talking about making babies... you shouldn't be focused on that until marriage, anyway! I digress.) Being fruitful refers to obtaining good moments, traits, and blessings that in turn multiply our life experience in a great way. These so-called strong and/or ruthless people were not born with that *"I don't need nobody"* mentality. They were taught by experience. Someone hurt them or someone they loved so deeply that now they have taken a position of coldness to the outside world. Some people are numb, not feeling anything from anyone as a defense mechanism. Others are in denial and stay in a state of naivety and make unwise decisions to continue associating with those that intentionally hurt them and betray their trust. To live freely in your true identity, you have to acknowledge the pains or mistakes that any betrayal activity may have left behind in your life. Even at your age you can beat betrayal at its own game. (Remember there are levels to betrayal and just like any video game, there are different skill sets you need to beat each level.) So, it's time to give BETRAYAL a **beatdown** so bad that it will think twice before trying to attack your identity again!

What does it mean to betray someone, anyway? Well, a few of the definitions, according to Merriam-Webster dictionary, are:

- Definition 1 - *To lead astray*
- Definition 2 - *To reveal unintentionally or to disclose in violation of confidence*

- Definition 3 - *To fail or desert especially in time of need*

In my opinion, the backstabber operates on three levels of betrayal. Level one is directly tied to definition one. When your "friend" has a history of leading you astray or off the path of who you really are and what you are about, then that person is not truly your friend. I don't care how long you have been friends or what wonderful things that they did for you. If you have attempted to stand up for yourself and brought the situation to their attention that you feel like something is not right and they wave it off like nothing happened...then, baby, WELCOME TO LEVEL ONE!

Fake friends are running rampant in the world today at an alarming rate! The main reason this epidemic is growing is because the victims of these fakers don't know their worth. If the person on the receiving end of a fake friend's shenanigans were to know that they don't have to put up with less than what they deserve, then, fake friends would fall off like a loose weave at the public swimming pool! People only do what you allow them to do. If you fight for your friendship by fighting for yourself, then the fake friend will either become a real one or will leave. You have to be smart and guard your heart. ANYONE that is willing to intentionally lead you astray from you being you at your very best needs to go! I don't care who they are. The skill needed to beat level one is simple: **Choose you.** Know your self-worth and that if anyone wants to continue to be your friend; then, they have to respect you and accept you as you are. In addition, real recognize real. Fake people run when confronted with truth and boundaries, but a real friend will try to understand where you're coming from and work on fixing that particular behavior or issue. Beating level one will be difficult for some, but it is necessary for your overall life advancement.

It is important that you are able to make friends. You may be different or even an outcast by someone's standards, but **you are not meant to be alone**. Make sure that if you have been stung by one too many fake friends that you recover. Learn from those ugly experiences so that you will know what the signs are as you go through life. Try not to shutdown because someone took advantage of your trust. The Bible says to "be not weary in well doing". In other words, do not get tired of doing the right thing. One of the hardest things about recovering from level one, is remaining friendly enough to give another person a chance to be your real friend.

I did not know how to properly recover from fake friends, and ended up becoming the very thing that hurt me. When I got to middle school, I wanted to shed my nerd persona. I wanted to be popular and I wanted a boyfriend…bad! The start of seventh grade brought about this brand new version of me that even I didn't recognize. I bought clothes and hung around girls that were of the "hoochie" culture. I unintentionally ignored my wonderful friends from elementary school that came over to this new school with me because they did not represent what I wanted to be. I made stupid decisions about my next set of friends based on low self-worth and previous acts of betrayal from people that weren't even my friends anymore.

Even though I was out there trying to "find myself" I lost the close relationship that I had with my best friend since first grade. There was no big argument or fight, but it was clear that I had lost some of her trust. She and I have always been cordial and are still very cool, but my own actions of being "fake" in the seventh grade caused me to miss out on growing older with my "sister" who had truly been my real friend from the start. I learned from that experience to never try to be anyone but myself. I am adamant on being authentic to every single person I meet, no matter what, as a result of becoming a betrayer to my best friend that school year. I still live with that to this day.

I tell my students all of the time to beware because you can be smart and stupid at the same time. When I was going through my seventh grade transformation I maintained my nerd like ways academically, but I was a plain idiot in my personal and social life. The things that I was involved in during the seventh grade (smh)… I never thought that I would ever be that stupid, but you live and you learn. As you go through life, young people, just know that YOU CAN BE SMART AND STUPID AT THE SAME TIME! Avoid it like the plague, please.

For some of us, it takes a lot to trust anyone. So, when we actually invite someone into our inner circle our expectation of them is to always value our trust by not betraying it. Level two is an obvious stage of betrayal as described in definition two. Definition two basically states a backstabber is capable of unintentionally revealing something or will disclose something in violation of confidence. It hurts beyond words when a close friend becomes a backstabber. Being the black jelly bean that I am, one experience from level two brought me pain that was so excruciating, so confusing, and super life changing.

Long story short, while in college one of my close friends began to change. I noticed sporadic little changes in her behavior towards me and I could not figure out why it was happening. Unsure of whether I had offended her, I attempted to be open and humble in our friendship so that I would not lose my good friend because of something that I may have said or done. Time went on and the little changes in her behavior became more frequent and more blatant. I was thoroughly confused because I had not committed any foul play or done anything wrong to her. I did not know what was going on. She was not acting like a friend anymore.

Then, one day it happened. She sat me down and explained to me that she hated me. Inside I could hear the loud thud of my heart drop! I loved her with all of my heart (hence, it dropped when hearing that she hated me). Though, I could not completely grasp the reasons or fully understand how our friendship stock had plummeted, we had an honest conversation and she was respectful as she shared her feelings. I learned that one of the reasons she hated me was that I was "me". I didn't do anything to her. I didn't necessarily offend her on purpose. She just didn't like "me" anymore. I loved her, but she hated me.

The skill needed to beat level two is: **Treat others the way you would want to be treated, no matter what**. Two things happened to me that day. One – I had matured to the point where I could accept that people change and that it is okay. I may have lost my friend officially that day, but I was proud of myself for not ever speaking badly of her because of the stuff she did to me and for always showing her nothing but love. My trust was betrayed in many ways throughout that experience, but I continued to do good regardless. I was not "weary in well doing". Many years later, she and I are still very cordial and I am very supportive of her endeavors. She is still dope in my eyes and I will always cherish the friendship we had prior to "the change".

Two – sometimes people will hate you because you are you. It's not always malicious. It's just real. Not everyone is going to like or love you. Oh, well. You cannot change who you are to make someone else feel comfortable. Matters not who they are or what role they may play in your life. That experience taught me how to be strong and hold true to my identity. I did not lose myself during that time. **Black jelly beans have to know how to be a part AND be apart unapologetically!**

Yes, friends are important, but not at the cost of your identity. Definitely be a part of a "family" or the "crew", BUT at the same time continue to be yourself even when that sets you apart from everyone else – and don't apologize for it! That is what it means to *"Be A Part and Be Apart Unapologetically!"*

Betrayal can be a beast! But, we've got to beat it at its own game. Level three is subtle, but the effect can knock you out if you let it. Definition three says that a backstabber will fail or desert you especially in your time of need. Essentially every level of betrayal that I have discussed has this element. However, the first two levels almost require someone to be close to you to commit the act. This level right here, though? Honey, anyone you are associated with can try you on level three.

Just shy of two years out of college, there I was on the top level of the aviation building standing in my newly bought professional ensemble. I was the new kid hired on the block and the youngest worker in the building. My boss's boss had called a meeting and my presence was required. He wanted to hear the recommendations from my department and the assigned collaborative department to this particular project. The assigned department's director and I had previously convened in preparation to give our sound report. She and I had this worked out and knew that there may be a possibility that the boss would not agree with one of our choices. We had strategized how we were going to present our argument and decided we would stick together. Together, we walked into the meeting with our materials. Together, we began to give our report. Then, the boss asked a question about one of our recommendations. Without hesitation or coercion, that director turned on me like a flapjack! She stood there while changing her position on our well-planned argument and threw me under the bus on top of all of that! It happened so fast, that I remember my mouth dropping open slightly. I quickly gathered myself and stood by what we agreed. I took it like the professional that I was outwardly, but inwardly I was going off! I was pissed!

How could this seemingly so sweet person just leave me out there like that at the first sign of trouble? She flat out deserted our plan and pushed me in front of the proverbial gun in case the boss started to shoot. Luckily, the boss didn't chew my head off. He just listened to me and did what he wanted to do in the end. When the meeting was over, I still had to work with this lady.

I could have allowed that experience to sour me on forming solid work relationships with all of the employees that I had yet to get to know. Again, I had been the "bigger" person and did not allow her experience to dictate how I would treat everyone else. The skill needed to beat level three is simple: **Don't let one experience ruin future opportunities.**

You cannot close yourself off from great relationships or opportunities because of the few bad apples that have betrayed you in life. I know that it can hurt when you are open and still have apprehension of people. However, try your hardest to keep being yourself. Don't grow cold. Don't become unfriendly. Use sound judgment and keep making connections. There will be times in your life when you will have friends that are closer to you than your own siblings.

It happened to me when I least expected it to when I joined a Christian women's group at college. To this day, most of the women from Women's Battalion for Christ are STILL my sisters. No matter the distance or time spent apart, I know that this "Prayer Diva" has a sister that loves me and will be there for me. I am special, but not that special. Keep being you and the real friends will come. Trust me!

## MISS BJB AFFIRMATION:

*I will not apologize for being myself, but I will be a great friend because I treat others the way I want to be treated: with respect and loyalty.*

# SEEKING SALVATION

*"Behold, I was shapen in iniquity;*
*and in sin did my mother conceive me.*
*Behold, thou desirest truth in the inward parts:*
*and in the hidden part thou shalt make me to know wisdom.*
*Purge me with hyssop, and I shall be clean:*
*wash me, and I shall be whiter than snow.*
*Make me to hear joy and gladness;*
*that the bones which thou hast broken may rejoice...*
***Create in me a clean heart, O God;***
***and renew a right spirit within me."***
*– Psalm 51:5-8,10 KJV*

The weight of my world was squarely on my shoulders bringing me down. Entering into my teenage years, I'd ultimately grown very tired of carrying the burdens I'd grown so accustomed to. What baffled me was that I could not pinpoint where my pain and depression came from, even into adulthood. I must admit I'd started searching for answers to alleviate my present state of despondence early on. However, I seemed to always feel hurt, even in times of celebration... genuine acts of kindness or fun eventually brought me to my depressed self, no matter how hard I tried to fight it. The things I used to solace my deepest pains were no longer working... I needed something more.

Enter Jesus Christ.

---

It was summertime 1996, at twelve years old I had already experienced a lot and internally wanted to experience something new. I can't remember the date exactly, but one day in August there was a knock at our door. My mother answered. There were two strangers' voices wafting through the apartment buffered by the screen door and my ears tried to latch on to the conversation. I couldn't make out what was being discussed. I moved on, but I really wanted to know what the discussion was about. Why? Because my mother let two perfect strangers who appeared to be "selling something" into her living room and listened to what they were saying for what felt like a very long time. Honestly, I HAD to know what the conversation was about. My mama NEVER let strangers like that in the house...EVER! I was eager to know what persuaded her to let them in. Finally, they left. My mother then announced to my brother and me,

*"You're going to church tomorrow."*

I couldn't believe it. You see, our family definitely believed in God. No doubt about it. However, we only went to church on Easter. Every blue moon, we'd attend church with our grandmother who interestingly was Catholic a good portion of my childhood. I went to the church services, but I never understood what was happening or even really connected spiritually. Needless to say, I wasn't ecstatic about going. On top of that, she was SENDING us to church with these people... she wasn't going with us. I felt some type of way, but at the same time I was hungry for something new and was willing to give this a chance – I was all in.

That fateful day began my journey to finding what I had been searching for. Every Sunday, my brother and I went to church with people who were once strangers that were now a part of our extended family. It was in that small church that we were effectively building a foundation of hope, righteousness and salvation. Up until that point, I had never been exposed. For a year, I soaked up everything I could about the Lord. I gave my life to God through Jesus Christ at the age of thirteen. I then received baptism by water and then later in the Holy Ghost on New Year's Day 1999. From that day to this one, even now as I write these words, I have faithfully lived my life as a believer in Jesus Christ and a servant of God. I know from whence I came and I know that I wouldn't be here today if God was not the head of my life. I was lost, but now am found.

### Why is this important for you to know?

It is important to know that it is ONLY through God's salvation that I am able to share my life's lessons with you. My intentions are to bring comfort and recommend solutions to very common issues. You will never understand or totally grasp the full capacity of the advice I give if I do not clearly explain that my help and the source of my triumphs solely come from the Lord. **I invite you to seek God for salvation today.** Romans 10:9-10 states that if you confess with your mouth and believe in your heart that Jesus is Lord, then you shall be saved. And just like that… the answer to all of your troubles is within you. It is literally that SIMPLE. Nothing stands in the way of you living free and as your best self, just give your life to Jesus. Why? Because Jesus is in you when you accept His salvation and life is worth living because He lives. Trust me, life is MUCH BETTER with Christ!

Though I've been saved and walking with Jesus for twenty years now, I found myself still struggling. In certain situations, I was still feeling alone in a crowded room. Over time, I discovered that this "walk" with Christ steadily evolves as I strive to become more like Him daily. At twelve, I'd finally found what I was searching for. More than a decade later, He was still searching ME to make me better. God loves us so much that He won't let us sit in our poop. Yes, I meant to write that. POOP! Imagine getting a brand new wardrobe, jewelry, new house, the works…but still soiled in your underwear. Even though no one can see, you're still dirty inside in your most private place. Sometimes, there's not even a smell…just skid marks of poop that only you know about.

In the epic poem, *"Free from Debris"*, I expressed my thoughts about my journey of how I finally got clean from my innermost pains. Transparency was very important to portray in this piece as it aided me in my healing while writing it. It is very lengthy, but remember I am attempting to address 30+ years of pain. As a matter of fact, it took me 3 ½ years just to finish it! Several times I had to stop writing because I wasn't ready to face a particular pain. Like those skid marks in underwear, you can conveniently forget they exist until you deliberately decide to investigate and thoroughly clean them.

**MISS BJB AFFIRMATION:**

*I have a friend in God and He truly loves me. Every answer I can ever need is in His son, Jesus Christ. I will seek Him when I need help.*

# FIGHTING THE FEAR FACTOR
# IN FORGIVENESS

*"Nay, in all these things we are more than conquerors through him that loved us." –Romans 8:37*

All my life I've had to fight…just kidding, sort of. Life for me has been good, actually. Even growing up in Desoto Bass Courts was cool for me. It was a rough environment, but my mother was dope in how she was able to raise my brother and me in a spirit of excellence and order despite the outside chaos. Though she brilliantly made me feel secure in our outward space, I had severe reservations in my inward spaces that even she could not straighten for me. As a child, I constantly observed people. I was very shy, so this way was how I got to know what a person was about before I emotionally attached myself to them. This was my signature defense mechanism: observation for survival. I have the ability to read people without them ever speaking a word to me directly. I honestly feel like God gave this tool to me at an early age so that I would not so easily get caught up in the very present dangers in the world. I had a pure heart and He thought it best to protect it.

Nevertheless, I had fear. It real live gripped me at my core and controlled my thoughts, actions and emotions. Similarly to my great aunt who seemed to have a fear about everything so much so that you could not sway her from her stance no matter what the logic, she allowed her fears to dictate how she lived her life. My fear is simple, but has made my life more difficult than it needed to be. **I have a fear of trusting.** Honestly, I even have trouble trusting God in some ways. It's a horrible thing to admit, but it is true. Not being able to trust people, things, systems and even good moments have robbed me from truly walking in my identity and receiving the good things that are meant for me to have. It took several years of soul searching, but I figured out where it came from. This fear took root on Friday, January 20, 1984…the day of my birth.

*Why was I so afraid of believing people? Why is it so hard trusting that they meant what they said even when they have never proven me wrong? Why was I outright always so completely uncomfortable when blessings were being bestowed upon me?*

That was the day my father decided to leave me. I am unsure of the physical date that he officially left, but after conversations with him, as an adult, I learned that mentally he had already checked out. I've been neglected and abandoned most of my life by the people that I feel like should have been there the most. The biggest source of my pain due to abandonment has been that my father was not fully present to love and raise me. On the day of my birth, he and my mother had some sort of disagreement that caused him to not pursue a hand in raising me. He chose to go on and live his life... without me.

He made his debut in my life at the age of nine. I was in the third grade. It was pizza day in the cafeteria. The day had started out perfectly with my favorite teacher and my favorite food. Back then, the school lunch was the bomb! I can still see and taste that pizza twenty plus years later. Mmm-mmm. During one of our fun lessons, my teacher got a call for Djuana to go to the office. Let me tell you, I was the perfect student! I never got in trouble, so I was very curious as to what this could be about. I literally had no clue. I walked the long, wide halls of Cleveland School for the Arts to the main office in the center of the adjoining building. As I began to approach the last set of stairs, I walked past some man sitting at an empty table in the middle of the hall. He was out of place and I had never seen him before. I dismissed the guessing game of who he could be and proceeded up the stairs to where my mother was sitting. I thought that someone must have died because my mother did not have a car and NEVER came to our schools unless there was an emergency. I braced myself and then she spoke…

*"Did you see that man downstairs?"*
*I said, "Yes", while wondering what could possibly be the importance of this stranger's presence in light of the pending emergency…*
*She then quietly blurted out, "that's your father!"*

My life changed at that point. You see, I went through my first years in life completely ignoring the fact that I was suffering. The old saying goes, "out of sight, out of mind" and that is exactly how I had addressed this issue. I just didn't. It became normal for me to not have a father. I didn't develop a longing for a daddy or even felt shortchanged because he was not around. In my possession was his name and his occupation, and I was satisfied with just that. Or so I thought. Seeing him and experiencing our very on-again, off-again father-daughter relationship has shined a bright light on some unwanted and unfair pain inside of me. I could no longer ignore the source of pain. I could not remain numb. The connection to my fear of trusting people had been exposed.

As I battled through all of the components of my pain in abandonment and neglect, God reminded me that He had not forgotten about me. The reason that blow to my life hadn't taken me out is because for about seven years or so prior to our first meeting, I had experienced the crumbs of fatherhood from my brother's biological father. Admittedly, he was not a perfect man, but the one thing that he did for me when he did come around was to acknowledge my presence. Mr. Spears was learning how to be a father to my brother while unknowingly was giving me the greatest gift of all: **showing me that I mattered.** He did not do anything extravagant, but he would always say hello. That meant the world to me! The grandest gesture I remember was when he was bringing my brother Christmas gifts and he gave me one, too. He gave me a stuffed koala bear. It was gray with a little white fur in the ears and it wore a yellow-patterned bow tie. I promise to you that that bear stayed with me for years! I thank God for the seed of acknowledgement placed in me by that man. As a little girl, I had a major deficiency that could drastically change my life's trajectory because my own father did not want anything to do with me. My brother's father didn't have to have anything to do with me and CHOSE to simply acknowledge my presence. It brings to tears to my eyes when I think of it. His memory will forever live on in me and I will always share the importance of just showing love to people because of what he did for me. May God rest his soul.

Growing up without a father contributed a lot to my shyness and to my insecurities. The abandonment left an indelible mark on my total being that resulted in this fear of trusting. In addition, it did not help that my family was already pretty broken and my single mother was never in a healthy relationship. These factors yielded the emotionally insecure person that I have become. Consequently, the undying fire that I have to make sure that those that suffer from abandonment are feverishly loved on within my resources is strong and unwavering! I know what the repercussions are to a young person that feels unloved and unwanted. I am here to tell you that you can conquer the pain! You have no power over the circumstances or the other person, but you can overcome your own pain so that you can be free. Please don't wait as long as I did to begin conquering this pain – I waited for twenty-three years before I began to actually address my issues. I had been afraid that trusting people and emotionally investing in them would cause them to leave me just like my father did. However, it proved that it did not protect me from getting hurt, but instead caused me more pain. It is through the example of my brother's father and several teachers after him that I adopted a new strategy to combat my fear. I learned how to channel my pain through the arts, how to show love and how to forgive.

I had to learn how to fight. I grew tired of allowing my fear to control me. So, God saw fit to lead my mother to send me to a school for the performing arts beginning in the first grade. Attending that school way across town literally helped to save my life. Life was throwing darts at me at an early age and I was already trying to ward off suicidal thoughts because of my circumstances. The arts were part of our academic structure and were integrated right into the curriculum. I was exposed to dance, gymnastics, drama, visual arts, creative writing, band, strings, piano and choir for free every week. I found out that being able to express myself through these mediums helped me to cope with my issues. I did not have to run to drugs, sex or rebellion in response to my pain. I played piano, wrote poems, acted in plays, clogged to country music, played violin in the orchestra, directed the choir, and even formed my own singing group. School was my outlet, my drug, and I had to have it!

Very seldom did I miss school, but those very few times brought literal tears to my eyes uncontrollably. I liken it to the pain of going through withdrawal. Today, I teach music (piano, singing, band, etc.) to willing and not-so-willing students privately and in inner city and charter schools. Learn from my life and discover a productive outlet to escape your pain. My vice lead me to graduating from one of the top performing arts high schools in the country, earning a college degree in music on scholarship, becoming an influential Airport Arts Coordinator, succeeding as a business owner, touring the country with a choir for free, and even writing this book. It is inevitable that pain and fears are going to come to us all, but it is up to us to learn how to fight through them. Carefully choose your weapons and avoid those that can cause more harm than good. Trust me, your pain can lead to a life that can be worth living as long as you fight for it!

Another tool that helped me to fight my fear was church. It was in church that I learned how to collaborate with others. I learned how to give. I learned the power of confession and testimony. I learned that loving someone can come without strings. Most importantly, I learned that forgiveness is the answer to total freedom. I have shared one of my greatest pains with you in this chapter, but I need to share with you how I got over it, how I continue to get through it. As I stated, forgiveness is the answer. Let me be completely real with you, forgiveness is not easy! It is a process that can be very painful in nature until you get used to it. Simply put, I learned to forgive the actions and the people that hurt me, the very things that caused me to be fearful in the first place. More than just my father, but many others and even myself have been on the receiving end of my forgiveness.

My mindset had to change in order for me to actually forgive anybody. I had to make forgiveness be about me. No longer did I want to choke to death because of a fear that dictated my life's choices. When I got older it became increasingly difficult to engage in the arts because my money was very tight and the opportunities weren't always there. It was just time. Unforgiveness was too heavy to continue to carry. It and my fear were going to kill my identity if I didn't do something about it. I would become a shell of a person with no life, no friends, and no peace. It was stopping me from living the life that I wanted. When I got engaged to be married, my fiancé (now husband) challenged me to tackle my issues or he wouldn't be able to marry me. That jolted me into action because I wanted to share my life with the person that loved me unconditionally. I was not willing to risk losing my gift, the love of my life. So, I reluctantly looked up to heaven and asked God to show me how to forgive. With each small step, I became freer. I told you that it has been a process, but I certainly am way better than I am now than what I was back then. You can be free, too, you know?

Forgiveness is not "hot" when it comes to the trends, but it is the hot ticket to living a life of freedom. You do not have to be old to forgive. You do not have to live a full-out beaten up life to begin the process of forgiveness. Practice letting go of things and people that hurt you and mean you harm. Decide within yourself that YOU ARE WORTH FIGHTING FOR! Your identity is directly related to how you conduct yourself. What are you afraid of? Not just what do you fear, but can you truthfully face yourself and live the life you imagine?

**MISS BJB AFFIRMATION:**

*I am not afraid! I will live life with freedom by forgiving myself and others. I am worth fighting for so that I can have the life that I truly want.*

# PRESSURES OF PERFECTION

*"And we know that all things work together for the good to them that love God and are the called according to His purpose."*

*–Romans 8:28 KJV*

Certain things can happen in life that can cause you to grow up sooner than expected. You may be in situations beyond your control where you have to be more mature than you are ready for. With no other options seemingly available, you have risen to the occasion. On top of all of that, you still have to be you. You still have to figure out who you are and what you want to do with your life at this age. It's a lot of pressure to get things right when you have to operate in more roles than your typical teenager of today. It is important for you to know no matter what pressure you may be experiencing in life that YOU ARE NOT PERFECT! And guess what? THAT IS OKAY!

*Have you been placed in a position where you have to balance more than homework and social media?*

*Do you feel like you are too young to be so overwhelmed or stressed out?*

*Do you feel the pressure to be perfect?*

No one can control the cards they've been dealt in life. That's understandable. Nevertheless, everyone is responsible for their own life and the only one that can live it is you. In this chapter, I simply want those of you that feel like life is "just too much" to know that you will get through this stage whatever it is!

I don't know if anyone has ever told you, but the older you get the harder life gets. It doesn't get any easier. There are still rules to be followed, no matter how stupid. There are still responsibilities to take care of even if you feel like it's not your fault. There are still deadlines to meet and "homework" to turn in. You will still have to share or stand in line. It gets harder because there is less grace or care for what you are going through when you're a full-fledged adult. In other words, I need you to figure out how to handle the pressures of life now so that you don't fold under the pressures when you get older.

I'm not trying to be negative, just real. I'm also not trying to negate what you're going through. I know that it is important to you and you have to figure out how to deal with it. But, dig your heels in, baby, and get through the issues you're having in life right now. It won't be easy.

It's not fair, but neither is life. You're stronger than your pressures. Find your strength by tapping into your identity.

**"Who am I?" you ask yourself.** That's a very good question. You need to figure it out. The sooner you learn who you are, what you like/dislike, and what you stand for, the better. The cards in your life's hand may not be great and the pressure to get stuff done or right may be strong, but if you know how to use what you already have with faith you will always win. You won't fold. As a matter of fact, do me a favor. **Learn how to pray and meditate, then write down what you discover.** Seriously! Through prayer and meditation, you can reflect in quiet and figure things out because your mind and heart is clearer.

**When you are walking in your authentic identity, you learn that you can only control what is in your power to control.** As long as you take care of your responsibilities the best way you can, then there's nothing more you can do. Stop stressing over things that are not in your power to control. Do you, boo! Then, take a deep breath and trust God with the rest.

It's really just that simple. Growing up in a single parent home is not easy for the eldest child. We have been assigned spoken and unspoken duties to perform to help maintain the household and even assist in the rearing of any siblings. I know. I lived that life. What I learned from maturing so early in life is that it is **my first responsibility to take care of myself**. If all that means is making sure that I participate in extracurricular activities that I actually like instead of what a relative may want, then that's what I mean. Learn how to be a kid in the midst of your responsibilities while you still can.

Lastly, just breathe! You are in a stage of discovery. You're learning. In learning, you may fail. THAT'S NORMAL. You're supposed to fail at things some times. As long as you learn from your mistakes and become a better person, that's all that matters. Don't put so much pressure on yourself to be perfect. Don't allow anyone to make you feel like you're not good enough when you're trying. I don't care who they are. **Just remember to control what you can control, breathe, and pray to God for strength and direction.** That's it. No, really. That's it.

**MISS BJB AFFIRMATION:**

*Being perfect is overrated. I am going to be me imperfectly and learn to take care of myself in every circumstance. I love who I am!*

# LEARNING 2 LOVE

*"You love me despite myself.*
*Sometimes I, I fight myself.*
*I just can't believe that You would have anything to do*
*with someone so insecure, someone so immature.*
*Oh, You inspire me to be the higher me."*

-Lauryn Hill
*(Lyrics from the song, "I Gotta Find Peace Of Mind" from Unplugged album)*

Rejected...

Ugly...

Lonely...

Broken...

Misunderstood...

Confused...

Angry...

Frustrated...

Depressed...

Victimized...

Alone...

These were all feelings I knew very well. I was very well acquainted with each and they seemed to always come visit me in this exact cycle over and over, like clockwork. The trouble with these visits was that they made me feel wrong for being myself. They made me feel like it was my fault that I was treated the way I was. I felt like I was not enough whenever this cycle of emotions began to take over my life. This was emotionally unhealthy and I was missing something. What was missing? Love. I kept missing when love would visit. I thought love had lost my address and didn't feel like I was worthy. Until one day I was shown that love was always there. I just didn't recognize it. I hadn't truly learned how to love…and it was time. Love was waiting for me and wanted the VIP treatment, to be my number one visitor.

The trouble with being a "black jelly bean" is that it becomes increasingly easy to spot when people don't like you, when they don't want you around. Black jelly beans seem to be a magnet for trials and tribulations. Our tough exterior is made from pain and experience. Inside, we seem to always be trying to hold it together. We wear masks of strength, but tears flood our inward parts. If the walls could talk or the car seats could speak, they would replay your wails and moans when each tear fell to hit your cheek. I wouldn't wish feeling unloved on my worst enemy! Black jelly beans have to work harder just to know when someone genuinely loves them. It is imperative for them to learn how to love themselves especially since it can seem like black jelly beans are more unwanted than others.

I am passionate about encouraging young people to love themselves and letting them know that they are loved. I love them! I do! I LOVE YOU, READER! I just want you to know that I mean it because there were unlikely people that God would send to me just to tell me that when I needed to hear or read it most. When I finished school, I rarely heard anyone tell me they loved me. I remember wearing my "it's all good" mask during a routine day at work in the YMCA after care program and one of the young participants just looked at me with their innocent eyes and simply said, *"Ms. DJ, are you okay? I love you."* It happened on more than one occasion. Sometimes it even came from the troublemaker child, but no matter which child it was I felt it and needed it. Their sincere words would snatch me out of depression and just like that I had more strength to get through my day. So, it's important to me. It's very important to me that young people know that I love them. It was through a child that I learned the power of love. There is pure power in saying, "I love you" and meaning it.

No one should have to ask someone to show them love. There are too many people like myself that have had to face this dilemma since they were a young person. The bottom line is not feeling loved causes deep emotional pain. It has always been difficult to explain to people how hard it has been to overcome my emotional pains. Despite the nature of some of my examples throughout this book, I feel as though that I had an enormously blessed life! I am fortunate to have what I have and to have been raised the way that I was with the people that God placed in my life. I am beyond grateful. I truly am. However, I have learned not to negate the fact that my pain came from somewhere. I did not make it up out of thin air. I have been to medical professionals and I have not been diagnosed with clinical depression nor do I have any chemical imbalance. The things that I have been through left things behind...they left these unhealthy, negative emotions.

To help remove the pain of the negative gunk in the corners of my heart and mind, I needed a solution. Getting to know God for myself has been HUGE in my life. It has literally saved me from going crazy! Prayer and studying the Word of God has been my saving grace. My relationship with God has been the only thing powerful enough to set right what has been wrong in my emotional life. God has been bigger than every situation and emotion I could have ever had. There is nothing and no one on Earth or beyond that can separate me from my belief in God because of that. I know Him for myself and know that He is able to restore love to you and make you whole. It's not a gimmick for me because I've tried Him for myself and I have no shame in suggesting that you try God, too! He works!

God protected me when I was boy-crazy and I was looking for someone to just like me at twelve years old. Not having my father around was catching up to me and I just wanted someone to want me. Though that may have been my desire, my mother had raised me to be a young lady and the standards that I'd adopted were embedded in me. I did not do anything that went against that upbringing, but my desire clouded my judgment on many occasions.

My body developed at an early age. I was wearing a training bra in the third grade and by the age of twelve I was well-endowed. Just walking through the neighborhood on a bright and sunny summer day from the bus stop someone noticed me and my body. I heard the booming deep voice of the onlooker yelling out to get my attention. I turned my head slowly to the right and there this grown man was sitting on the tiny porch drinking a can of beer that was nestled snugly in his left hand. The screen door revealed that the back door of this apartment was closed. Now, that was not typical during the summer time. None of the units at that time had air conditioning units. So, no one sat outside of their apartment with both doors closed, that's just not what we did around the Bass. This man was clearly not a resident of the apartment that he was chilling in front of. My limited survival instincts kicked in immediately and my thoughts were racing with ways of how to get out of this situation.

I slowly approached the porch leaving at least 4 grown bodies length of space between him and me. He asked for my name and I gave him one. Gina. That was the name on my neon canvas wallet. (There were never any products with my name on it, so I would pick what I liked.) There was no way I was going to give him my real name. He was a stranger. Stranger danger is what I was thinking. All I knew was that I didn't want to upset him because he was so much bigger than me.

Still trying to escape, I barely heard anything that he said. He went on saying whatever he was saying and this uncomfortable exchange seemed to last forever. At consistent intervals, I would naturally allow my eyes to search around my surroundings for a familiar face, a housing authority worker, or just any man that could rescue me from what felt like imminent danger. There wasn't another soul in sight. I felt unlucky. The hood was never this quiet during the summer. I had run out of options and felt I had no choice but to get out of this situation before something crazy happened.

My instincts were yelling at me to "get out now!" Consequently, I cut him off in his conversation and made up some excuse that I had to leave. Placing one foot deliberately behind the other, I slowly began to back up. Before I knew it I was booking it across the field, flying across the street to the next building, nervously putting the key in the latch and with everything I had slamming the door closed. Just as I closed the door, an unknown car suspiciously turned down my street fast. I knew it was him. I knew that he was looking for me. By the grace of God, I was safe. I knew it was God that got me out of there. I told my mother and she was ready to find and kill him. Lucky for him, no one was able to find that man and had not seen him around the neighborhood again.

Now, I wasn't looking for that kind of attention. I didn't want some older man trying to talk to me to violate me or worse. Shoot, on that day I was coming from summer camp I was wearing a French braid in my hair like one of those girls on the show *"Little House On The Prairie"*. I did not look like an adult at all. I was so confused. That's not the kind of love that I wanted.

Within just one month, I started middle school. I was going to be surrounded by boys my own age that didn't know me and I couldn't wait. Finally, I was going to get a boyfriend. I was determined to make it happen. I craved for male attention in the seventh grade, but it backfired. The boys I really wanted to like me only saw me as friends while the ugly boys that didn't care about their grades were all over me. Every period when the bell rang, there was some little ugly boy trying to get my attention inappropriately. I'd been smacked on my booty several times. A boy with stank breath attempted to kiss me on my lips. Thank God I turned away when I did even though he managed to brush his crusty lips across mine for a nanosecond. (Frowning and shuttering now while thinking about it.) Walking down the hall to the cafeteria with the lunch crowd, a cuter boy that I was crushing on had came behind me and put his arm around my shoulders. I was in heaven until I realized that he was using the fingertips of his right hand to fondle my right breast. He was so slick about it that it even took me a minute for it to register that it was even happening. With no shame whatsoever, he did that right there in the hallway amongst everybody. There were times when a group of them nasty boys would chase me trying to lift up my dress or skirt. Yes, a group. I admit that I may have dressed a bit enticingly, but I did not want nor did I deserve to be treated like a piece of meat.

Seriously, I did not want THAT kind of attention. None of these instances made me feel more loved or wanted. Instead I felt unworthy of love and used up. Why couldn't one of them just ask me out on a date? Why did it have to only be about the physical? I didn't understand it and did not have the maturity to know how to get the respectful treatment that I actually deserved which was far better than what I was receiving.

It wasn't until I walked down the aisle of my yellow school bus during dismissal that I finally understood that this was a real problem and needed to end. In my own little world, wearing a regular fit pair of jeans and a basic tee shirt, I walked down the aisle to sit in my bus seat. While walking

I felt a hand grab me in my vaginal area out of nowhere. I looked down and saw the boy grin at me as he quickly took his hand away. He did not apologize or look away or even talk to me. Somewhere on the inside he must have felt that it was okay to grab my groin like a piece of fruit and did just that. That was the lowest point of my middle school social life. My self-worth had hit rock bottom.

Without putting up a fight, I allowed these boys to commit these acts to me in front of people. They showed no remorse and took no thought to how this would affect me. They didn't care. I was too ashamed to fight back or even tell anyone back then. For years, I kept this to myself until a student that I taught in high school heard my testimony and asked how I was able to overcome being sexually assaulted. I had never looked at it that way. I did not think that I was a victim of any form of sexual abuse because these were my peers. I thought that it was my fault because I really wanted a boyfriend and I wore short skirts, so hey. Whatever happened to me was a result of horny teenage boys being horny teenage boys. Once I said that out loud, a student who is also a survivor of sexual abuse had confirmed that that was exactly what a victim of sexual assault feels like. Holy cow, I was sexually assaulted. Sad to say, but until that very moment I had no idea that sexual assault was what I had been through.

As if that wasn't enough, I was just short of being kidnapped right in front of our neighborhood early one morning waiting for the school bus. Now, I told my mama about this one! It happened fast and I was super confused. I was confused because I had rid myself of my "hoochie-fied" clothes and was wearing gym shoes, a red crew sweatshirt and red sweatpants. I had opted for the plain look and I looked it. All of a sudden, this no-window-having-but-in-the-front van pulled up at the bus stop where I was and he rolled down the window. Again, my instincts were like "be on guard". This man wanted me to get in his van for a "good time". I replied, "no, thank you" as if being polite was going to lessen my chance of being abducted. Once again, I began looking around for my bus. It seriously chose the wrong day to be running late! The man gave up his attempts and pulled off without warning! I let out a big breath of relief and noticed that I was shaking. I prayed to God to keep me safe and was instantly angry that that was the morning my mother was not looking out the screen door watching me. As soon as I had decided to go back home, the bus turned the corner. I went on to school, but as soon as I got home I told my mother everything. This mess had to stop and thank God it did.

The decision was made to search for love in God when I was thirteen years old. I took steps toward Him and He kept showing me what love truly is. When I began the eighth grade I felt like a completely different person. For the first time, I was sure of myself. I felt beautiful. I was comfortable in my own skin and only allowed the right kind of people and activities into my atmosphere. I began my journey to take control of my life. From eighth grade to the present day, I have purposefully been learning how to love myself.

I started in the Word of God with learning what the definition of love is. God is love. I may sound like a fanatic at this point, but I can't help myself. I only shared a tweet-sized portion of my journey. That negative cycle of emotions that constantly visited me surely began to break down when I began to seek after God.

I had tried a few other things before and they just didn't work. But, with God's love and guidance I was no longer plagued by my troubles or feelings. I had figured out how to recognize love when it was visiting and I learned how to give love VIP treatment over the other emotions.

The bottom line was and still is that I need love. We all do, especially the black jelly beans. Therefore, I had to learn that I couldn't rely or wait on someone else to give me love. Before, I desperately wanted someone to show me love, but my life experiences made me feel like I didn't deserve it. I'm so glad that I was wrong! Not only did I need love, but I was worthy of it as well.

God has ALWAYS loved me and He was waiting for me to recognize it. He was powerful enough to show me how to overcome my darkest trials and my deepest depressions because He loved me. He was powerful enough to teach me how to love myself because He wants me to live an abundant life. No matter what tragedy you may go through in life or how hurt you may feel, you have to know that you are not abandoned. Trouble won't last always. You have to know that God loves you and He wouldn't bring you this far to leave you.

Now, it is our responsibility to continuously learn to see ourselves the way God sees us so that we can fully learn how to love ourselves the way God sees fit.

**MISS BJB AFFIRMATION:**

*I love me because I am on this earth to be unique fearfully and wonderfully the way God made me. I owe it to myself to show ME love so that I am able to effectively love others.*

# I ACCEPT…

*"Knowing others is intelligence; knowing yourself is true wisdom. Mastering others is strength; mastering yourself is true power."*
*-Aristotle*

Feeling alone in a crowded room is just part of the package if you're a black jelly bean. Though I accept that others may not notice me or even completely understand me, I will no longer FEEL alone. My life's journey has shown me that I truly am never alone. There is someone out there that gets me. Someone out there loves me. Someone out there wants me. Even when I can't find a single soul to fit the bill, I know for sure that GOD DOES without question.

Black jelly beans are meant to be different and set apart. Black jelly beans are NOT meant to be alone or be perfect. Life may be hard at times and you may even be hated, BUT your uniqueness and inner strength make you a world changer. If trials are present in your life, remember that they won't last always. Keep doing you and come out on the other side so that you can be a light for someone else. Your tests will be your testimony just like mine has been for me.

I understand that hurt people hurt people and that when I forgive those that have hurt me then I will be free. Walking in my true identity means that I will lose some, but I will win more. Spending more time on knowing and loving myself is not selfish, but essential to my life. As a matter of fact, I accept that it is more important for me to love me before I expect for someone else to do it.

I accept me when no one else can see my worth!

I accept me when life is beating up on me!

I accept me when I try to love and they betray me!

I accept me when those that I need the most leave me!

I accept me when the pressures of life feel unbearably unfair!

I accept me when I feel some type of way... it is okay!

I accept me and believe that God loves and will never leave me!

I accept and refuse to ever let the true me go no matter what challenges I may face!

Black jelly beans are meant to be *"a royal priesthood, a holy nation, a chosen generation and a peculiar people" that is to show forth the praises of God who has called us out of darkness into His marvelous light.* (I Peter 2:9

paraphrased) Thus, it makes sense for people to not understand us without getting to know us. I accept that it is my duty and my pleasure to keep being me!

No more mistaken identity because I accept being **Miss BJB**!

To know me is to love me...comprehension is the key!

# THE MISS BJB PLEDGE

I PLEDGE TO ALWAYS BE MYSELF. I WILL BEGIN TO DO WHATEVER IS NECESSARY TO MAKE SURE THAT I AM EXACTLY WHO GOD HAS CALLED ME TO BE. I DARE TO BE DIFFERENT AND FULLY UNDERSTAND THAT I DO MATTER! I WILL WORK HARD TO OVERCOME MY OBSTACLES AND WILL GROW FROM MY PAIN. FROM THIS DAY FORWARD, I WILL BE MYSELF IN THE FACE OF EVERY CHALLENGE.

Be A Part & Be Apart
UNAPOLOGETICALLY!

SIGNATURE: _____

DATE: _____

# MISS BJB AFFIRMATIONS

# MISS BJB AFFIRMATIONS

## CHAPTER: *DESTINED 2B DIFFERENT*

*I am who I am comfortably and I absolutely love my identity. It is necessary for me to be me so that I can leave my unique mark on the world. I, boldly, will be different and stand out amongst the crowds.*

### WRITE YOUR OWN:

_____

_____

_____

## CHAPTER: *MISS ME…THE MISCONCEPTION*

*I will fight for my true identity. The words and actions of others will not change my being, but it is allowed to positively shape my being. No matter how misunderstood, misinterpreted, or misrepresented that I may be, I will ALWAYS strive to be ME!*

### WRITE YOUR OWN:

_____

_____

_____

# MISS BJB AFFIRMATIONS

## CHAPTER: *K(NO)W NEGATIVITY*

*Today is the day that I will give the stiff arm to any words of negativity that have the potential to injure me instead of grow me. I will speak life into my life and commit to knowing that there is <u>no excuse</u> for being negative.*

## WRITE YOUR OWN:

_____

_____

_____

## CHAPTER: *SUICIDE IS SERIOUS*

*I matter! I was given life so that I can <u>live it</u> and one day will leave a great legacy in the world. I matter!*

## WRITE YOUR OWN:

_____

_____

_____

# MISS BJB AFFIRMATIONS

## CHAPTER: *LIVING WITH LOSS*

*I have not been abandoned even when loved ones leave. I recognize that they are with me in spirit and their memory is my strength when I am low. God has never and will never leave me. I am strong!*

## WRITE YOUR OWN:

_____

_____

_____

## CHAPTER: *BEATING BETRAYAL*

*I will not apologize for being myself, but I will be a great friend because I treat others the way I want to be treated: with respect and loyalty.*

## WRITE YOUR OWN:

_____

_____

_____

# Miss BJB Affirmations

## Chapter: *Seeking Salvation*

*I have a friend in God and He truly loves me. Every answer I can ever need is in His son, Jesus Christ. I will seek Him when I need help.*

### Write Your Own:

_____

_____

_____

## Chapter: *Fight The Fear Factor In Forgiveness*

*I am not afraid! I will live life with freedom by forgiving myself and others. I am worth fighting for so that I can have the life that I truly want.*

### Write Your Own:

_____

_____

_____

# MISS BJB AFFIRMATIONS

## CHAPTER: *PRESSURES OF PERFECTION*

*Being perfect is overrated. I am going to be me imperfectly and learn to take care of myself in every circumstance. I love who I am!*

## WRITE YOUR OWN:

_____

_____

_____

## CHAPTER: *LEARNING 2 LOVE*

*I love me because I am on this earth to be unique fearfully and wonderfully the way God made me. I owe it to myself to show ME love so that I am able to effectively love others.*

## WRITE YOUR OWN:

_____

_____

_____

## VIEW MORE FROM TRU TALENT PRODUCTIONS

### VISIT WWW.TRUTALENTPRODUCTIONS.COM

*Currently offering the following Services:*

**Tru Music** – Private Piano Lessons

**Tru S.T.A.R.T. Life Coaching** –
*"Get your LIFE from VISION to FRUITION!"*

**Tru Divas Club –** An Encouragement Community for the
Proverbs 31 Woman

**MISS BJB - THE SPOKEN WORD MOTIVATOR** is
also available for Speaking Engagements,
Life Coaching, and
Performing Inspiring Spoken Word Poetry

Find out more about Miss BJB at
**www.TruTalentProductions.com/MissBJB** or
**www.MissBJB.com**

Contact Djuana Ross for booking information at
**DRoss@TruTalentProductions.com**

www.ingramcontent.com/pod-product-compliance
Lightning Source LLC
LaVergne TN
LVHW021357080426
835508LV00020B/2324